A Beginning-to-Read Book

A Visit to the Police Station

by Mary Lindeen

NORWOOD HOUSE PRESS

DEAR CAREGIVER, The *Beginning to Read—Read and Discover* books provide emergent readers the opportunity to explore the world through nonfiction while building early reading skills. The text integrates both common sight words and content vocabulary. These key words are featured on lists provided at the back of the book to help your child expand his or her sight word recognition, which helps build reading fluency. The content words expand vocabulary and support comprehension.

Nonfiction text is any text that is factual. The Common Core State Standards call for an increase in the amount of informational text reading among students. The Standards aim to promote college and career readiness among students. Preparation for college and career endeavors requires proficiency in reading complex informational texts in a variety of content areas. You can help your child build a foundation by introducing nonfiction early. To further support the CCSS, you will find Reading Reinforcement activities at the back of the book that are aligned to these Standards.

Above all, the most important part of the reading experience is to have fun and enjoy it!

Sincerely,

Shannon Cannon

Shannon Cannon, Ph.D.
Literacy Consultant

Norwood House Press • P.O. Box 316598 • Chicago, Illinois 60631
For more information about Norwood House Press please visit our website at
www.norwoodhousepress.com or call 866-565-2900.
© 2019 Norwood House Press. Beginning-to-Read™ is a trademark of Norwood House Press.
All rights reserved. No part of this book may be reproduced or utilized in any form or by any
means without written permission from the publisher.

Editor: Judy Kentor Schmauss
Designer: Lindaanne Donohoe

Special thanks to Chief Joe Miller and the Village of Palos Park.

Photo Credits:
Phil Martin, cover, 1, 3, 4-5, 6-7, 12-13, 16-17, 18-19, 22-23, 24-25, 26-27;
Shutterstock, 9, 10, 11, 14; iStock Photo, 8, 20-21, 28-29; Palos Park Police
Department, 15

Library of Congress Cataloging-in-Publication Data
Names: Lindeen, Mary, author.
Title: A visit to the police station / by Mary Lindeen.
Description: Chicago, IL : Norwood House Press, [2018] | Series: A beginning
   to read book | Audience: K to grade 3.
Identifiers: LCCN 2018010167 (print) | LCCN 2018004467 (ebook) | ISBN
   9781684041763 (eBook) | ISBN 9781599539119 (library edition : alk. paper)
Subjects: LCSH: Police–Juvenile literature. | Police stations–Juvenile
   literature.
Classification: LCC HV7922 (print) | LCC HV7922 .L5645 2018 (ebook) | DDC
   363.2–dc23
LC record available at https://lccn.loc.gov/2018010167

Hardcover ISBN: 978-1-59953-911-9   Paperback ISBN: 978-1-68404-167-1

A Beginning-to-Read Book

A Visit to the Police Station

by Mary Lindeen

NORWOOD HOUSE PRESS

DEAR CAREGIVER, The *Beginning to Read—Read and Discover* books provide emergent readers the opportunity to explore the world through nonfiction while building early reading skills. The text integrates both common sight words and content vocabulary. These key words are featured on lists provided at the back of the book to help your child expand his or her sight word recognition, which helps build reading fluency. The content words expand vocabulary and support comprehension.

Nonfiction text is any text that is factual. The Common Core State Standards call for an increase in the amount of informational text reading among students. The Standards aim to promote college and career readiness among students. Preparation for college and career endeavors requires proficiency in reading complex informational texts in a variety of content areas. You can help your child build a foundation by introducing nonfiction early. To further support the CCSS, you will find Reading Reinforcement activities at the back of the book that are aligned to these Standards.

Above all, the most important part of the reading experience is to have fun and enjoy it!

Sincerely,

Shannon Cannon

Shannon Cannon, Ph.D.
Literacy Consultant

Norwood House Press • P.O. Box 316598 • Chicago, Illinois 60631
For more information about Norwood House Press please visit our website at
www.norwoodhousepress.com or call 866-565-2900.
© 2019 Norwood House Press. Beginning-to-Read™ is a trademark of Norwood House Press.
All rights reserved. No part of this book may be reproduced or utilized in any form or by any
means without written permission from the publisher.

Editor: Judy Kentor Schmauss

Designer: Lindaanne Donohoe

Special thanks to Chief Joe Miller and the Village of Palos Park.

Photo Credits:
Phil Martin, cover, 1, 3, 4-5, 6-7, 12-13, 16-17, 18-19, 22-23, 24-25, 26-27;
Shutterstock, 9, 10, 11, 14; iStock Photo, 8, 20-21, 28-29; Palos Park Police
Department, 15

Library of Congress Cataloging-in-Publication Data
Names: Lindeen, Mary, author.
Title: A visit to the police station / by Mary Lindeen.
Description: Chicago, IL : Norwood House Press, [2018] | Series: A beginning
    to read book | Audience: K to grade 3.
Identifiers: LCCN 2018010167 (print) | LCCN 2018004467 (ebook) | ISBN
    9781684041763 (eBook) | ISBN 9781599539119 (library edition : alk. paper)
Subjects: LCSH: Police–Juvenile literature. | Police stations–Juvenile
    literature.
Classification: LCC HV7922 (print) | LCC HV7922 .L5645 2018 (ebook) | DDC
    363.2–dc23
LC record available at https://lccn.loc.gov/2018010167

Hardcover ISBN: 978-1-59953-911-9   Paperback ISBN: 978-1-68404-167-1

312N-072018
Manufactured in the United States of America in North Mankato, Minnesota.

Look at these cars.
Who works in this building?

Police officers
work here.

This is a police
station.

Sometimes officers work at their desks.

They use computers.

They talk to people on the phone.

Sometimes officers
drive police cars.

These cars are ready to go.

Sometimes officers ride police bikes.

These bikes are ready to go.

Sometimes officers work
with police dogs.

This dog is ready to go.

Some officers even work
with police horses.

The horses live and
eat at the station.

The officers can eat
at the station, too.

Here is their kitchen.

Here are their lockers.

There is one locker for each officer.

This is the
police chief.

He is in charge.

This is the police
operator.

She answers
the phone when
someone calls
for help.

Then she tells
the officers who
needs help.

And she tells them
where to go.

The officers are
in their cars.

The red and blue
lights come on.

They go, go, go!

...READING REINFORCEMENT...

CRAFT AND STRUCTURE

To check your child's understanding of the organization of the book, recreate the following chart on a sheet of paper. Read the book with your child, and then help him or her fill in the top part of the chart with what he or she learned. Work together to complete the bottom part by writing questions your child still has about police stations:

What I Learned	<ul><li></li><li></li><li></li><li></li></ul>
What I Want to Know	<ul><li></li><li></li><li></li><li></li></ul>

VOCABULARY: Learning Content Words

Content words are words that are specific to a particular topic. All of the content words for this book can be found on page 32. Use some or all of these content words to complete one or more of the following activities:

• Help your child look up the words in the dictionary, then tell the meanings in his or her own words.

• Have your child make up riddles about the words.

• Ask your child to find the words in other reading materials in your home.

• Help your child find the commonalities between or among the words. Ask: *Which word goes with _____?*

• Have your child define words by category and one or more attributes (example: *a horse is an animal you can ride*).

FOUNDATIONAL SKILLS: Consonant Digraphs

Consonant digraphs are formed when two consonants together make a new sound: *sh* (ship), *th* (thumb), *wh* (white), *ch* (chip), *ck* (duck), *ch* (watch), *ph* (photo). Have your child say the following words and tell which consonants create the digraphs. Then have them find other words in the book with consonant digraphs.

these	who	this	with
the	when	them	where

CLOSE READING OF INFORMATIONAL TEXT

Close reading helps children comprehend text. It includes reading a text, discussing it with others, and answering questions about it. Use these questions to discuss this book with your child.

- What is one piece of equipment used by a police officer?
- Why might some police officers ride bikes?
- Where might police horses live at the police station?
- Who do you think has the most important job at the station? Why?
- What might happen if the police operator did not answer the phone?
- What does it mean when the red and blue lights come on in a police car?

FLUENCY

Fluency is the ability to read accurately with speed and expression. Help your child practice fluency by using one or more of the following activities:

- Reread this book to your child at least two times while he or she uses a finger to track each word as it is read.
- Read the first sentence aloud. Then have your child reread the sentence with you. Continue until you have finished the book.
- Ask your child to read aloud the words they know on each page of this book. (Your child will learn additional words with subsequent readings.)
- Have your child practice reading this book several times to improve accuracy, rate, and expression.

··· Word List ···

A Visit to the Police Station uses the 68 words listed below. *High-frequency words* are those words that are used most often in the English language. They are sometimes referred to as sight words because children need to learn to recognize them automatically when they read. *Content words* are any words specific to a particular topic. Regular practice reading these words will enhance your child's ability to read with greater fluency and comprehension.

High-Frequency Words

a	even	on	them	when
and	for	one	then	where
are	go	people	there	who
at	he	red	these	with
blue	help	she	they	work(s)
can	here	some	this	
come	in	tell(s)	to	
each	is	the	too	
eat	look	their	use	

Content Words

answers	chief	kitchen	operator	sometime
bikes	computers	lights	phone	station
building	desks	live	police	talk
calls	dog(s)	locker(s)	ready	
cars	drive	needs	ride	
charge	horses	officer(s)	someone	

··· About the Author

Mary Lindeen is a writer, editor, parent, and former elementary school teacher. She has written more than 100 books for children and edited many more. She specializes in early literacy instruction and books for young readers, especially nonfiction.

··· About the Advisor

Dr. Shannon Cannon is an elementary school teacher in Sacramento, California. She has served as a teacher educator in the School of Education at UC Davis, where she also earned her Ph.D. in Language, Literacy, and Culture. As a member of the clinical faculty, she supervised pre-service teachers and taught elementary methods courses in reading, effective teaching, and teacher action research.